Contents

Any words appearing in bold, **like this**, are explained in the Glossary.

Cotton and its properties

All the things we use at home, school and work are made from materials. Cotton is a material. We use cotton for many different jobs. Most cotton is used to make **fabrics**. Cotton fabrics are made into things such as shirts and sheets. We also use cotton to make cotton wool, and even tea bags.

If you look at cotton fabric through a microscope you can see lots of cotton fibres.

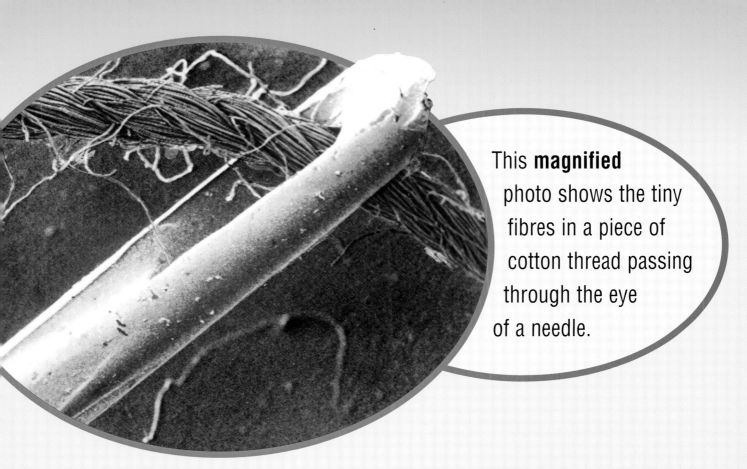

This **magnified** photo shows the tiny fibres in a piece of cotton thread passing through the eye of a needle.

Properties tell us what a material is like. Cotton is made up of bendy **fibres** like hairs. One property of cotton is that it is **flexible**. The fibres are just a few centimetres long and much thinner than the hairs on your head. They are white or slightly grey. Other properties of cotton include feeling soft and soaking up water.

Don't use it!

*The different properties of materials make them useful for different jobs. For example, cotton soaks up water so it is no good for making **waterproof** clothes.*

Where does cotton come from?

Cotton is a **natural** material. It comes from the cotton plant. After a cotton plant has flowered it grows pods with seeds inside. The pods are called **bolls**. They split open to let the seeds out. The cotton **fibres** that we use are joined to the seeds. They help the seeds float through the air when they are blown from the pod by the wind. There are long fibres called **lint** and short fibres called linters.

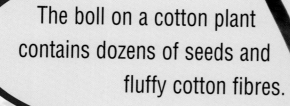

The boll on a cotton plant contains dozens of seeds and fluffy cotton fibres.

These cotton plants are ready for the cotton fibres to be picked.

The cotton industry

We use more cotton to make **fabrics** than any other material. Cotton growing is a huge **industry**. Most of the cotton we use is grown on farms in the south of the USA and China. Cotton grows best in places where there are lots of warm sunny days and plenty of rain.

7

Preparing cotton

When the **bolls** on cotton plants open the cotton **fibres** are ready to be harvested. On large cotton farms machines collect the fibres. The machines move along the rows of cotton plants pulling off the cotton fibres. On small cotton farms the cotton is often picked by hand.

A cotton harvesting machine pulls fibres from the plants with spiky wheels.

A bale of cotton contains the fibres from many thousands of plants.

After harvesting, the cotton fibres are still attached to the seeds. The fibres and seeds are pulled apart by a machine called a cotton gin. The fibres are also cleaned and dried. Then they are bundled together into huge **bales** ready to be sold.

More cotton products

Cotton fibres are not the only part of cotton plants we use. Cotton seeds contain valuable oil, which is used for cooking. After the oil is taken out, the rest of the seed is made into food for cattle.

Cotton yarn

Most cotton that is grown is made into long strings called **yarn**. Cotton **fibres** are very thin and not very strong, but they cling together well. Cotton yarn is much thicker and stronger than the cotton fibres. Cotton yarns are used to make cotton **fabric**. They are also used for stitching fabrics together and for **embroidery**. This kind of yarn is also called thread.

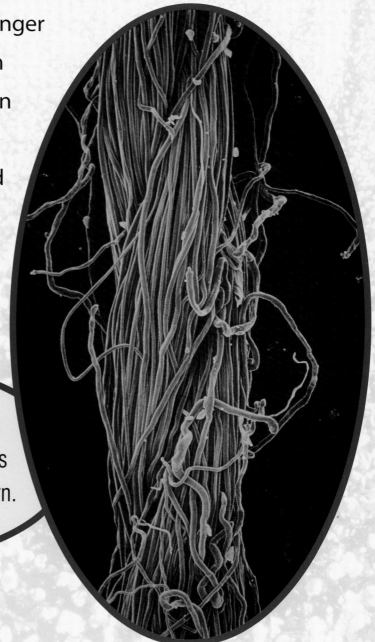

Through a microscope you can see the cotton fibres twisted together in cotton yarn.

Cotton fibres are spun into yarn by spinning machines.

Cotton yarn is made by spinning. The cotton fibres are lined up so they all point in the same direction. They are gathered together and then spun round so they twist tightly together. The fibres cling to each other. This is how long lengths of yarn are made from short cotton fibres.

Cotton in the past

Scientists think that people started using cotton as a material about 5000 years ago. People made cotton yarn and fabrics by hand. The first spinning machine was invented about 700 years ago. The machine made it much quicker to spin cotton yarn.

Cotton fabrics

Most cotton **yarn** that is spun is used to make cotton **fabrics**. Cotton **fibres** make soft, comfortable fabrics. There are many different kinds of cotton fabric. Some are made with very thin yarns. These fabrics are thin and smooth to touch. Some T-shirts are made of thin cotton fabrics. Other cotton fabrics are made with thick yarns. These fabrics are thick, strong and feel quite rough. Overalls are made of thick fabric.

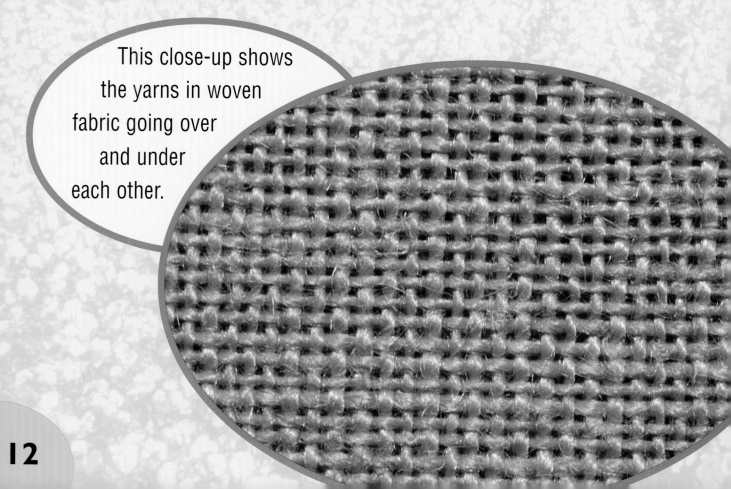

This close-up shows the yarns in woven fabric going over and under each other.

In this close-up photograph of a knitted fabric you can see the loops of yarn.

Weaving and knitting

We make cotton yarns into fabrics by **weaving** and **knitting**. To weave a fabric, lengths of yarn are passed over and under each other. A machine called a **loom** weaves fabric very quickly. Knitted fabrics are made from loops of yarn. Knitted fabrics can stretch more than woven fabrics.

Don't use it!

Cotton fabrics are not fireproof. Cotton can catch fire easily and burn quickly. So we cannot use cotton where it might catch fire. For example, we would not make a blanket for putting out fires from cotton.

Cotton colours

Natural cotton is white or light grey, but cotton **fabrics** come in many bright colours and interesting patterns. The cotton **fibres** in them are coloured with **chemicals** called **dyes**. We can dye cotton fibres before they are spun into **yarn**, or we can dye a length of yarn. We can also dye a piece of fabric. Dye soaks into cotton fibres very well because cotton soaks up liquid. When the dye dries, the colour stays.

Iron-on transfers have dyes that soak into the cotton when they are heated by an iron.

This woman is weaving a pattern with coloured cotton yarn.

Making patterns

Patterns on cotton fabrics are made by printing and **weaving**. Printing on fabric works just like printing on paper. The colours are made by dyes in the ink. Woven patterns are made by using different coloured yarns in the same fabric. The way the lengths of yarn go over and under each other changes the pattern. **Looms** automatically weave patterns as they make fabric.

Cotton clothes

Most cotton **fabrics** are made into clothes for us to wear. The **properties** of cotton fabrics make them good for clothes. Cotton fabrics feel soft next to your skin. They also soak up sweat from your skin, keeping you dry. Dirt and grease cannot cling on to cotton **fibres** very well, so cotton clothes are easy to wash. People like the **natural** look of cotton, too.

Thin, loose cotton clothes keep you cool by letting air flow around your body.

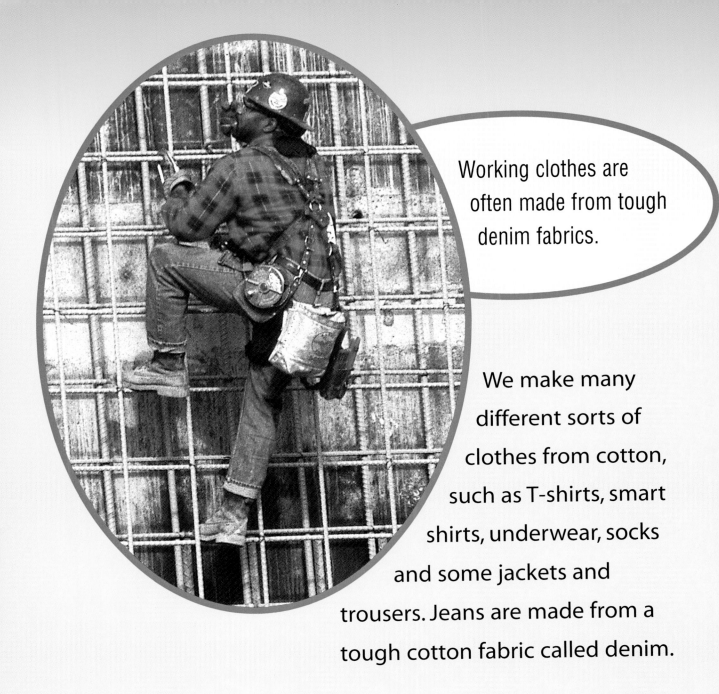

Working clothes are often made from tough denim fabrics.

We make many different sorts of clothes from cotton, such as T-shirts, smart shirts, underwear, socks and some jackets and trousers. Jeans are made from a tough cotton fabric called denim.

Don't use it!

Cotton fabrics are not suitable for making every sort of clothing. For example, cotton fabrics are not very warm to wear. They do not dry very quickly, and wet cotton clothing can make you chilly when it is cold.

More cotton fabrics

We use cotton **fabrics** to make many other objects apart from clothes. Cotton is used to make bed clothes because is it smooth and soft. We also make furnishings such as curtains and lamp shades from coloured and patterned cotton fabrics. We make tents, deckchairs and sun shades from thick, strong cotton fabrics.

Cotton sheets, pillow cases and duvet covers are soft and comfortable.

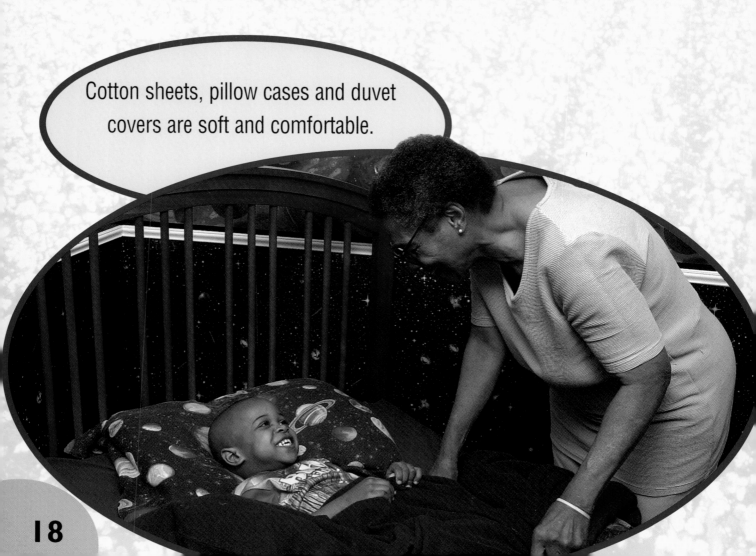

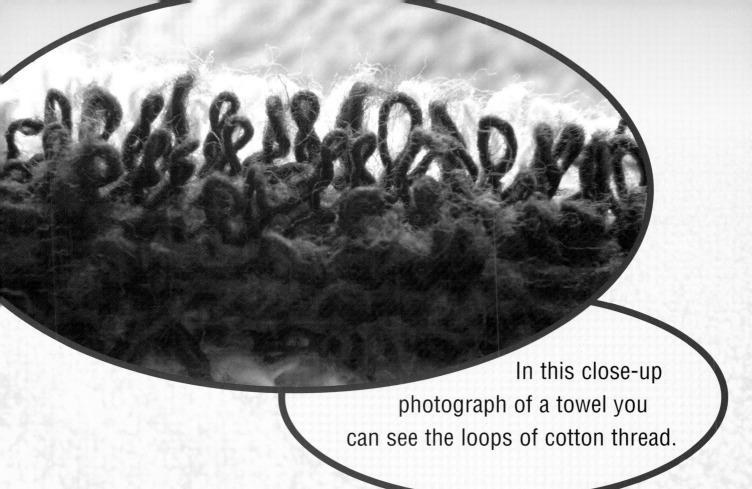

In this close-up photograph of a towel you can see the loops of cotton thread.

Soaking up water

We make bathroom towels and tea towels out of cotton fabrics because cotton **fibres** are so good at soaking up water. Towels are **woven** with loops of fluffy **yarn** on each side so they dry you quickly. If you look closely at a towel you can see the loops of yarn.

Don't use it!

Cotton is not strong enough to make things that are handled roughly. For example, we do not make big sacks from cotton. We make them from tougher plant fibres such as jute.

Decorating with cotton

Cotton threads and **yarns** are thin, strong and easy to bend. These **properties** make cotton good for making **fabrics** for decoration. **Embroidery** is decorating plain fabric by sewing thread into it. Different colours of cotton thread are used to make colourful pictures. The thread is thin so very detailed pictures can be sewn. Embroidered cotton fabrics are used to make tablecloths and wall hangings.

Cotton fabric is pulled tight over a frame to make it easy to stitch.

Cotton lace can be **dyed** different colours.

Lace making

Lace is a type of fabric. It is made by twisting and **weaving** together many different cotton threads. Patterns are made by lines of thread and also by leaving holes in the fabric. Cotton thread makes soft, delicate lace. Lace-making takes lots of skill. Lace can be used along the edges of other fabric for example, a cotton handkerchief. Crochet is similar to lace-making. Lace makers also use silk and linen to make lace.

Making cotton better

Sometimes cotton is not exactly the right material for a job. However, we can still use cotton by making its **properties** better. Cotton **fibres** are often mixed with other sorts of fibres in **fabrics**. The fabric then has the properties of both sorts of fibres.

Labels on a piece of clothing show what kind of fabric it is made from.

50% COTTON
50% POLYESTER
Wash Separately
Cold Water
Do Not Bleach
Tumble Dry Low

This jacket is made from polyester-cotton, so it is hard wearing.

Finishing cotton

*Cotton fabrics can be made better by treating them before they are used. This is called finishing. For example, waxed jackets are made of cotton soaked in wax. This makes the cotton completely **waterproof** because water cannot flow through wax.*

A material called **polyester**-cotton is popular for making clothes. It is a mixture of cotton and polyester, which is a sort of plastic. Polyester-cotton fabrics are easier to wash and iron than pure cotton fabrics. Cotton is also mixed with **nylon** to make fabrics that are more hard-wearing than pure cotton fabrics. Socks made from cotton and nylon soak up sweat, stay in shape well and last a long time.

Cotton padding

Very short cotton **fibres** are called linters. They are bundled together to make cotton padding. Padding is very soft and spongy. It is weak, so it is easy to pull apart. It also soaks up water and other liquids very well. Cotton padding is very comfortable to sit on. Car seats and cushions for furniture are often filled with it.

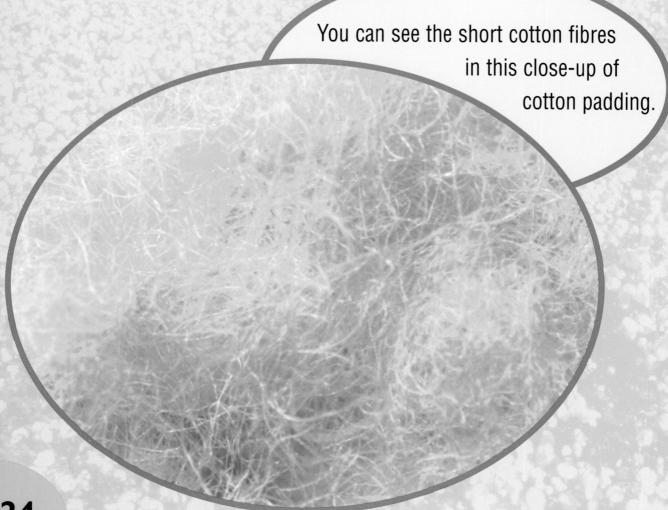

You can see the short cotton fibres in this close-up of cotton padding.

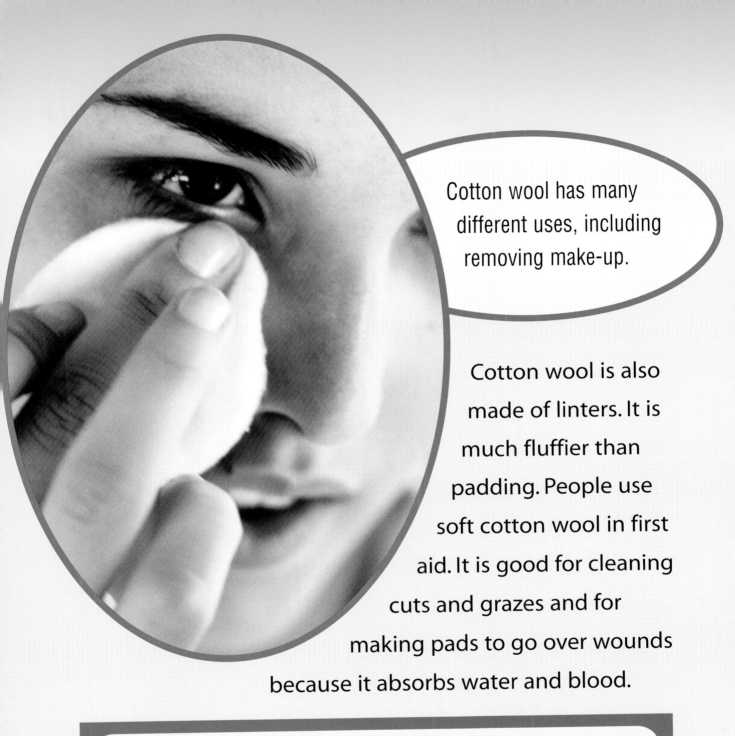

Cotton wool has many different uses, including removing make-up.

Cotton wool is also made of linters. It is much fluffier than padding. People use soft cotton wool in first aid. It is good for cleaning cuts and grazes and for making pads to go over wounds because it absorbs water and blood.

Don't use it!

*Linters are no good for making **yarn**. The yarn would be very weak because the fibres are too short to cling to each other well. Linters are also turned into a **chemical** called cellulose, which is used to make **artificial** fibres.*

Throw-away cotton

Cotton is quite a cheap material. Some cotton **fibres**, **yarns** and **fabrics** are made into things that we use once and then throw away. They are **disposable** things. Cotton wool is disposable. So are cotton pads for putting on wounds. We also make disposable things, such as tea bags, from cotton.

The fabric of a tea bag is like paper. There are spaces between the fibres that let water move in and out of the bag.

This man is tearing up cotton rags which will be made into paper.

Cotton in paper

Cotton can be made into paper by pressing wet fibres together into a thin mat and letting it dry. Normal paper is made from fibres from wood. Paper made from cotton is stronger and lasts longer than normal paper. Cotton paper does not tear easily. Paper for bank notes contains cotton fibres.

Don't use it!

*Some things made from cotton are disposable, but many are not. We do not use **woven** and **knitted** cotton fabrics to make disposable things. These fabrics are expensive to make. Cotton wool and cotton paper are much cheaper to make, so we do not waste much money when we throw them away.*

Cotton and the environment

Cotton is a **natural** material from plants. Cotton should never run out because we can keep growing more. We can throw it away because it **rots** naturally. However, growing cotton and making cotton into clothes and other things can harm the environment. For example, so much water is needed to grow cotton on farms that rivers can dry up. The **chemicals** we use to bleach and **dye** cotton can also poison rivers if they are not thrown away carefully.

Cotton clothes can be different colours and styles and all can be recycled.

Old cotton clothes make useful rags and cloths.

Recycling cotton

We can use some cotton again instead of throwing it away. This is called **recycling**. Old cotton **fabrics** are pulled apart to get the **fibres** back. The fibres are used to make new cotton things such as cotton cleaning pads, dusters and rags. Scraps of cotton are also used to make paper. You can reuse cotton at home, too. Use old T-shirts as dusters and rags for cleaning instead of buying new cloths.

Find out for yourself

The best way to find out more about cotton is to investigate cotton for yourself. Look around your home for things made from cotton, and keep an eye out for cotton through your day. Think about why cotton was used for each job. What **properties** make it suitable? You will find the answers to many of your questions in this book. You can also look in other books and on the Internet.

Books to read

Science Answers: Grouping Materials, Carol Ballard (Heinemann Library, 2003)

Discovering Science: Matter, Rebecca Hunter (Raintree, 2003)

Science Files: Textiles, Steve Parker (Heinemann Library, 2002)

Using the Internet

Try searching the Internet to find out about things to do with cotton. Websites can change, so if one of the links below no longer works, don't worry. Use a search engine, such as www.yahooligans.com or www.internet4kids.com. For example, you could try searching using the keywords 'cotton **industry**', '**yarns**' and 'lace'.

Websites

A great site, which explains all about different materials:
http://www.bbc.co.uk/schools/revisewise/science/materials/

A fun site that explains how cotton is grown and used:
www.cottonsjourney.com

Glossary

artificial anything that is not natural

bale large bundle of material tied together with ropes

boll seed pod of a cotton plant

chemical substance that we use to make other substances, or for jobs such as cleaning

disposable describes an object that is designed to be thrown away after it is used

dye coloured chemical that soaks into a material to change the colour of the material

embroider to make patterns or pictures in a fabric by sewing coloured thread into it

fabric flat sheet of bendy material such as cotton or leather

fibre long, thin, bendy piece of material

flexible able to bend

industry group of organizations that do the same job. For example, iron making is an industry. So is coal mining.

lint long cotton fibres

liquid substance that takes the shape of whatever container it is put into

loom machine used to weave fabric from yarn

knit make fabric from yarn by making linked loops

magnify make something look much larger

natural describes anything that is not made by people

nylon artificial material, like plastic, that can be made into fibres

polyester artificial material, like plastic, that can be made into fibres

property quality of a material that tells us what it is like. Hard, soft, bendy and strong are all properties.

recycle to use material from old objects to make new objects

rot to be broken down

waterproof describes a material that does not let water pass through it

weave make fabric by pressing lengths of yarn over and under each other

yarn long, thin piece of material made by twisting fibres together

Index

How We Use

Cotton

Chris Oxlade

Schools Library and Information Services

www.raintreepublishers.co.uk

Visit our website to find out more information about **Raintree** books.

To order:
☎ Phone 44 (0) 1865 888112
🖹 Send a fax to 44 (0) 1865 314091
💻 Visit the Raintree bookshop at www.raintreepublishers.co.uk to browse our catalogue and order online.

First published in Great Britain by Raintree, Halley Court, Jordan Hill, Oxford OX2 8EJ, part of Harcourt Education.
Raintree is a registered trademark of Harcourt Education Ltd.

Editorial: Nick Hunter
Design: Kim Saar
Picture Research: Heather Sabel and Amor Montes de Oca
Production: Alex Lazarus

Originated by Ambassador Litho Ltd.
Printed and bound in China by South China Printing Company

ISBN 1 844 43267 X (hardback)
08 07 06 05 04
10 9 8 7 6 5 4 3 2 1

ISBN 1 844 43277 7 (paperback)
09 08 07 06 05
10 9 8 7 6 5 4 3 2 1

British Library Cataloguing in Publication Data
Oxlade, Chris
How We Use Cotton. - (Using Materials)
620.1'97
A full catalogue record for this book is available from the British Library.

Acknowledgements
The publishers would like to thank the following for permission to reproduce photographs:
Corbis pp. **5** (Ron Boardman/Frank Lane Picture Agency), **6**, **7**, **9** (Roger Ball), **21**, **27** (Paul Almasy); Drk R. Kuyper p. **13**; Getty Images pp. **25** (Stone), **26** (Photodisc); Harcourt Education pp. **18** (Robert Lifson), **22** (Jill Birschbach), **28** (Jill Birschbach), **29** (Jill Birschbach); Image Works pp. **8** (Jack K. Clark), **11** (Topham), **20** (Syracuse Newspapers); Jonah Calinawan pp. **14**, **19**, **23**; Mark Dixon p. **12**; Peter Kubal p. **4**; Photo Edit p. **16**; Science Photo Library (Photo Researchers Inc) p. **10**; Tom Pantages p. **24**; Visuals Unlimited pp. **15** (Jeff Greenberg), **17** (Tom Uhlman).

Cover photographs reproduced with permission of Corbis (Lance Nelson) (top) and Corbis (bottom).

Every effort has been made to contact copyright holders of any material reproduced in this book. Any omissions will be rectified in subsequent printings if notice is given to the publishers.

The paper used to print this book comes from sustainable resources.